collective madness

poems by

adrienne danyelle oliver

Finishing Line Press
Georgetown, Kentucky

collective madness

for the 80%

Copyright © 2022 by Adrienne Danyelle Oliver
ISBN 978-1-64662-737-0 First Edition
All rights reserved under International and Pan-American Copyright Conventions. No part of this book may be reproduced in any manner whatsoever without written permission from the publisher, except in the case of brief quotations embodied in critical articles and reviews.

ACKNOWLEDGMENTS

I would like to acknowledge the spaces where my work has previously been published. I am grateful to Nomadic Press for publishing "a poem about fibroid tumors" in *Patrice Lumumba: An Anthology of Writers on Black Liberation* and in *the body has memories* (Nomadic Press, 2022), in which "belly" is also published.

Publisher: Leah Huete de Maines
Editor: Christen Kincaid
Cover Art: Kalari Flotree
Author Photo: Simone Anne Lang
Cover Design: Elizabeth Maines McCleavy

Order online: www.finishinglinepress.com
also available on amazon.com and bookshop.org

Author inquiries and mail orders:
Finishing Line Press
PO Box 1626
Georgetown, Kentucky 40324
USA

Table of Contents

:a poem about fibroid tumors 1

:black and white 5

:a cherry wood desk for writing... 6

:well-intended white folk 7

:on cannibalism.. 14

:surreal killer 16

:u deter us 18

:sub-myoo-KOH-zuhl.. 19

:echo 21

:belly 25

:queen mother 28

For all its fraudulence, however, race is a myth with teeth and claws, one that continues to tear bodies apart. …Until we recognize it for the collective delusion it is, it might as well be real.

—Resmaa Menakem, *My Grandmother's Hands: Racialized Trauma and the Pathway to Mending Our Hearts and Bodies* (p. 68)

:a poem about fibroid tumors

I.
the black woman body carries Afrika
in her womb
and this womb remembers

      cargo of bodies
   waiting to be crucified
or set free

      the body remembers how the strongest cargo
      knowing freedom is death
      jumped and returned to the ship
as angels
      while the deceived
      with eyes adjusted to darkness
      nose to the smell of despair
cultivated another strength
to pray for the angels to save them

my belly carries
        ghosts
        a returning

a watching
        over corpses
              and living bodies—

II.
I learned
to shrink as an accommodation
shoulders
developing knots
from squeezing closed
    around lungs
      pumping restricted breaths

when the white lady doctor
tells me I need to have
a hysterectomy
I overstand that
what she is really telling me
is this

carried over
in a ship named Good Intent
the body been wearied by this
voyage
and white lady doctor don't understand
how an Afrikan w(omb)und stretched
across the Atlantic and
crucified
can
still   bring forth life
can
                      commune
            with
hope

I listen to white lady doctor
read her intentions
and her right to vote
as well intended
                but know she will never
understand the plight of
                Mother Afrika to African-American
battered
       terrorized
              dispossessed

tearsinblackboycoffinsandblackgirlchurchbombings/
turnedbloodintheFergusonstreets
because it's cotton picking season in
MississippiandAlabama/Missouri
Minnesota
Georgia
Texas
and everywhere else

like slave ship my body
carries: life and death
       rotting carnage and breathing captive
suffers: the most damage
knows: "it"—she—the universal black womb is crying out in
chorus.

and the white lady doctor's response
ishurriedsuddenly after 400 years:

rip out the wo(und)mb
toss her out
in a hazardous materials
bag

matter-of-factly she offers black
hat solutions
as if talking to a child
anticipating doves

I have two other options
     besides the illusionist's show
                                   one.
I can live with bleeding
bleeding
bleeding
bleeding
blood in the   stre/she/ets

                                    two.

I can be cut
with her help   have tumors removed
empty the ship in Amerikkka
"land of the free"
and wh/try ignoring the
smell of death
sweep remnants
of clinking shackles
to corners in the
fields of my mind
but
cotton picking season
is year round in
America's soul

and what harm is damaged cargo
in a ship on fire?
a ship full of cancer
cells
breeding ghosts

still I decide
to dance with the haunted
wo(und)mb on
troubled water.

:black and white

first, i want to say i'm sorry.
the Black lady doctor

i'm glad i hadn't read the note
it said the cyst was 10 cm and life threatening.
basically, it was saying that i could die over an email.
i'm glad that i heard it from my black doctor first
before reading it in black and white.

what an amazing difference it made
to receive my test results from a black woman.
not to overgeneralize
because i can remember another time
in my life
when a black woman doctor
did not have the best bedside manner.
so there was definitely something
about this particular black woman
in this moment.

:a cherry wood desk for writing

when i got this apartment i was acting
like i was moving back into a house
cue *The Jefferson's* theme song
'cause finally—after roommates and ikea tables—
i was getting my own
space
turned out a cherry oak, corner desk
in the furniture showroom
wasn't corner furniture in any of my rooms
it was a centerpiece that yelled
look at me
louder than anything else.
after much agony i decided to give it away.
i tried to sell it online
first
but everybody wants something for nothing
after two weeks
i determined to get more space in my bedroom, deleted the price
updated the ad on Letgo:
free cherry wood, corner desk
i made a commitment to measure my space
think about dimensions
next time
so I wouldn't have to give away
what had been so good to me
now i'm always measuring everything
to avoid agony
of giving something treasured away
before its season
it was a lesson well learned.
now i'm not sure if i'm writing about the desk anymore.

:well-intended white folk

                        free cherry wood, corner desk
                            i put an ad on freecycle
                    after not getting responses on letgo
                    i don't know what made me do that
                        probably a memory of having
                                 given things away
to people i thought were well-deserving of something free
                              black folks, brown folks
                            hungry students in debt
end up this well-to-do white couple answered the ad. from
                                         danville.
i remember that danville was a place for the well-to-do cause
just so happen i was interviewed for a job there at the athenian
                                           school
          this secondary school cost college tuition to go there
                        and the interview was grueling
                               i had to teach a class and
                        be interviewed by a table full of
                               private school students
                      well-manicured, bright-eyed, and
                         speaking in good SAT vocabulary
                 it's probably a good thing i wasn't hired there
                 my public school diploma, chipped fingernails
                            and southern grammar
                                already at odds with
              what could have been my death sentence
                     the couple from danville arrives
                        i meet them at the front door
                     to take them up the elevator
        to my floor—buzzer to let in guests long broken
      the three of us cram into the 1950s style, tiny elevator
           then my (feeling) only slightly bigger bedroom
                  the husband takes the desk apart
                   and the wife does the carrying
         the taking away of each piece bit by bit

down the elevator
out the door
to the vehicle that will take
them back to danville
i stand over the white man
kneeling over the desk
until he unscrews
the last wooden leg
from the desk's overturned top
he rests a hand on my bed to catch his breath
to lift himself back up to standing
i feel the sudden urge to run
to reach for the wooden leg
to explain that I'm leaving the room
to take down the last piece of the leg

on my way down in the elevator
i regret leaving the white man alone in my apartment
but am glad to have some air
some space from whatever it was that triggered
my urge to run away from being alone
with him in a bedroom

when i reach the car
the woman is busy
rearranging the disassembled pieces
neatly into the back of a sedan
we decide to go back up
help her husband bring down the desktop
the smooth wood carved into a perfect corner
the last piece

i hold the elevator
and the words back:
*i didn't want no white folks
coming to take nothing else
help with nothing else
help still feels like a house slave
an air conditioned cotton field—
a taking away from me
but i'm desperate for air
in this summer heat*

my tiny bedroom had been overcrowded
by the big desk overseeing big ambitions
with no investors,
no space for dreaming
the bedroom is more realistic after
the desk gone
after we each have
taken a corner of
the big desktop
taken the elevator down
together in awkward silence

the bedroom is more realistic after
the desk gone
empty spaces feel more familiar
than big desk dreams
than the noise of aspiration
crowding out haunted solitude

after they left I lit incense
eager to use the new
wooden
incense holder i had bought
from the nepalese store on park avenue

after leaving the doctor's office
this umpteenth time
after discussing
alternative child bearing options
a donor egg donor sperm
and if that didn't work
a surrogate or adoption

now here I was in the empty
sitting on
the bed breathing in
the new empty space
now here I was in the empty
communing with echoes of the talk
in my doctor's office

i noticed that the incense box
was shaped like a miniature coffin
this was my first day sitting with
the incense box
this was my first day sitting without
the big desktop full of promise
this was my first day sitting with
my true feelings about the echocardiography results
my true feelings about donor eggs
and carrying a baby without my DNA
the feelings were unsettling
yet relieving, in a strange way—
it was a conversation this time
a letting down easy
rather than a breakup by betrayal
an invitation to still be friends
with promise
still it didn't change
that this was an ending

the all of this converged together
as cause for a funeral
i had a coffin
a reason to mourn
and painful truths to accept

my womb wasn't going to be a spring flower
in this summer field of my life
in this box
where the executive desk don't fit
in an overpriced studio existence
in this box
where epigenetic sexual trauma
echoes in the ancestral womb

the serendipity of the incense box
being coffin-shaped
the empty space
pallbearing
the conversation about infertility
the white people coming to
take away
my baby dreams
the all of this converged together
as cause for a funeral

i had every intention of writing a eulogy
a poem
about unpacking
the well intention of white folks
a poem
about how whiteness
navigates systems
like a white marriage
filing taxes

claiming insurance
or surfing a listserv
looking for something free
and paying private school
tuition
a poem
about how many black mothers
die in childbirth
in hospitals
after living a whole lifetime in midwives' hands
a poem
about black wombs and infertility
a poem
about family stories of white men
putting their hands on our beds
a poem
about how the fact that whiteness
and all its well intentions
no matter how unwanted or unwarranted
are accepted
because we are suffocating
a poem
about what we didn't choose
about how it crams us up into
tight spaces not big enough
for our dreams
yet greedy
for our nightmares
a poem
about the all of this
converging together
as cause for procession

it was going to be a good poem
but
i'd grown so weary
from the elevator ride
from the cramped space
from the hand on the bed
from the mourning
from the painful truths to accept

that
instead of writing a poem
i sat on the edge of the bed
I watched the sunset and
incense wispily float
through the holes in my
incense box,
holes shaped like lace or
bullet holes
allowing smoke
from a burning gun
to seep through

:on cannibalism

I.
when the settlers arrived
they didn't know how to
cultivate the land
so
they ate indigenous bodies
dug open their graves
and never fully learned
to quench the hunger
for flesh

II.
when the slaves arrive
the settlers know how to eat food
by now
but the appetite for flesh remains
remains
they tear open
into
legs they spread
like mayonnaise
before biting
planting a seed through their saliva
making the hunted a hosting body

III.
the babies got his grey eyes
ghost skin
tough on a mama to know
her baby born
from all seven sins in his Bible
She tried to run away once
sunk bare feet into mud
a dark brown welcoming
earth

Ran in the rain
with the sin baby
in arms
head bustled into
warm breasts

Ran and ran and ran and ran
until her foot got caught
on something sharp
and tight
like a lion's mouth
closed in around her
feet
no not feet
foot
right foot
and still to this day
her feet cramps up
terribly
when even thinking about
running
the trap mark
now an echo in her flesh

IV.
I eat a piece of my own foot
swallow my baby
to savour him
I've inherited this
now I can't run anymore

:surreal killer

And after all that running
I find my body

in a waiting room.

on a church pew.

under a dark moon.

longing
to be mothered
to be a mother
for mothering.

the baby i swallowed whole
is an old spiritual—a tree planted by the waters/a great gettin up
morning—
now drowning in the Atlantic
there is no
running left
to do with an ocean
between us and no legs to swim
i leave my longing to
be mothered to be
a mother for
mothering
as a haunting at the shores
while the remains of my body sit
still in the waiting room
filled with wooden benches and
cold eyes focused forward
my spirit leaves the room full
        of longing

—too many of us there
gettin our wings cut off
and bled into an unmarked
trap [grave]
set for anchoring us
down

:u deter us

a black woman is sitting alone
in a studio apartment
wondering where her man is
who has yet to materialize
wondering where the food for
the tumors growing in her uterus
is grown from
wondering who tends that field inside her
wondering if the ache
in her back
in her shoulders
in her neck
are from today, yesterday
or a delayed reaction from
her mother's or her
mother's mother's affliction(s)
wondering if
her body
(-) minus the booty
the breast
the bodacious hips
is black enuf for the matrix
(+) plus the scars
the aches
the barrenness of
her womb is
woman enough
wondering if
according to this gospel
she can ever be saved

:sub-myoo-KOH-zuhl

Stomach
    an organ of which membership
    belongs to the digestive
    system
    muscle [lining] acid
    movement

        Would you make my potatoes dairy free?
        That'll be easier on my stomach.

          i forgot
          i'm not supposed to say any lines [requests]
          stomach fills up with [words] unsaid

Heart
    an organ of which membership
    belongs to the cardiovascular system
    muscle [lining] blood

        When I was 12...
          i forgot   *was it*   *[1992]?*
        When I was 16...
          i forgot *i'm not*
          13...   *[remembering 1919].*
        present day =
          a part i can no longer remember
          with words
          heart fills up with _____

Womb
    sing us a line of song
        escape   system
      rope [lining] acid
          scream about
              whisper about
                  [moan about]

Lungs
        breathe from stomach
        give   a i r   to
        heart   fill [feel]
        voice in the womb [with singing]

:echo

I.

a nice white couple comes
to pick up a Black woman's cherry
wood desk
shaped for a corner
while in the corners
of her mind
a story needs to be set free
they pick up her desk
on her first day of bleeding
a day for lighting incense
for the story between her hands
in her mind
she frees herself from
        corners
into the center
where incense wafts to the ceiling
alongside interrupted dreams
where her postcard from the other side
was delivered
where she signed her freedom papers
in a past life
a premonition wafts
in dreams filled with night sweats
behind windows
facing an industrial sunset
pipe dreams killed with pipes smoked
planted
burning trees
cousins of trunks bearing
strange fruit
blowing smoke over bridges to history

II.

> *when the Black lady doctor explains*
> *that my womb bleeds into*
> *the wrong places*
> *and that the body attacks the blood*
> *I overstand that*
> *what she is really telling me*
> *is this*

heart
       has run
to love
       in all the wrong places
been attacked
               hardened
into an eternal echo

The radiologist says   *It's hard to hear*
through the scar tissue in my belly
she had pressed and pressed
onto my abdomen

Back in the kind doctor's office, she asked
                Can I see your belly?

Unable to move my lips anymore
I raise my shirt

      they keep using me
      same incision

              At least it heals up nicely

Yes, the scar was smoothed last heartbreak
shovel smoothed over the dirt
patted into a mound
under kind
fluorescent

> *she explains tenderly*
> *that attacks harden the blood*
> *into*
> *an endometrioma*
> *a six-syllable word*
> *foreshadowing*
> *a fifth surgery*

Inside myself I tell her
    it will be okay
assuringly this time
    it will be okay
to convince myself this time
    it will be okay
               usually you have painful periods
    No, my pain is an echo now

muted

                whiplashed
   from
whips
   lashed
           I/she was raped
                and kept the baby
a slow bleeding
a letting go
a deep inhaling of
dreams
wafting slowly up and through
carved holes in a coffin-shaped box

III.

a sun sets in West Oakland
with cranes and bridges
in the sky
and she reminds herself
that death is a letting go of
I in exchange for we—

we stand in dreams wafted
through coffins overseeing
slaves trapped in cherry groves
holding at gunpoint
all contemplating
a return
corners where
strange fruit is
rotting
while black and white postcards
of the lynching show eyes full of wonder
and delight

our freedom papers
are stories about all that blood
are big mama's hands
washing the red moon off
and hanging our white dresses
in the mo(u)rning sun to dream.

:belly
    a meditation on loving the scars beneath her shirt

index fingers
    make a "V"
    right fingernail left outer tip
    left fingernail right outer tip
kissing
+
thumbs
    bent at right knuckle
    bent at left knuckle
    nail beds touching

=

a heart shape

made with her own hands
this heart lives over her belly
the throughline is a scar beginning beneath breastbone below her
beating heart and ending at her pelvis
bone
the throughline is this scar
penetrated with scalpel
four times

in the black space
between counting

      10   9   8   7   6   5

to waking up
connected to an

                                        IV

she imagined that her skin was pinned
to a cold surgical table
her organs fully exposed
now laying here past midnight
she approaches   4 a.m.
like morning
       eyes wide open
palms flat
rising on inhale
then sinking

                         index finger + thumbs = heart

hand
      heart

               over

                     belly

c   h   i   l   d   's   p   o   s   e

                 beginning of

                   loving
                   line
                   down
                 center(ed)
                   her

/

right palm over dark splotch
where
ostomy bag
used to be

+

left palm over two dark scars
branded like dice
where catheter for bladder
used to be

=

and yet
she
is
light

:queen mother

You reading this
You love me because
I am
a survivor
I bleed
I sweat
I breathe
the pride of Africa
I am
God's love
when my womb grows
My skin splits and a new birth happens
babies cry like trumpets
light of the earth
my baby daddies
are scattered in the Eastern wind
chilled in the underworld
of the West
I stand from North to South
stepping
in to raise kingdoms
My scars—
        creation story
My tears
        compounding dirt into diamonds
My heartbeat
        oxygenating the earth
My veins
        rivers connecting the oceans

I breathe
        you live
I breathe
        you live
I breath
        you live
until we die

You cannot live
without me
your mother
your sister
your nurturer
your life giver

without me
the earth is void

With Thanks

I am holding a huge amount of gratitude for God and the story that is my healing. I'm grateful for all of the people and experiences that made this chapbook possible. I acknowledge my mother, Barbara; sister, Angela; and countless family members and friends who support me in my creative work and healing journey. My acknowledgements would be incomplete without an expression of gratitude for the work of Eastside Arts Alliance's Holla Back Open Mic in housing the collective that is the Patrice Lumumba writer's workshop in East Oakland, CA. This space has nurtured the work published here. I also acknowledge San Francisco's Museum of the African Diaspora for debuting early versions of this work on their Poet's Corner blog. I would also like to acknowledge the San Francisco Bay Area Generations Reading Series for showcasing this work and the Furious Flower Poetry Center for Black Poetry for the fellowship that lit the fire. I'm also grateful for Gwendolyn Mitchell, whose editorial guidance helped shape the narrative arc of the poems, and Patrick Oliver, whose publication guidance helped foster this project. I am also grateful for the advance reviews and praise shared graciously from writers I admire: Lauren K. Alleyne, Thea Matthews and Tongo Eisen-Martin—three remarkable poets; and author Faith Adiele, whose memoir on uterine fibroids, *The Nigerian Nordic Girl's Guide to Lady Problems*, inspired my own treatise on fibroids. Another artist I would like to acknowledge is my friend and artist Kalari Flotree for the beautiful book cover art. I have tremendous gratitude for this beautiful artwork. Last but certainly not least, I'm grateful for Leah Huete de Maines and the team at Finishing Line Press for the design featuring this art and for the publication of *collective madness*.

adrienne danyelle oliver is a poet-educator from Little Rock, Arkansas based in the San Francisco Bay Area. Her previous work has appeared in *Storytelling, Self, Society* (Wayne State University Press, 2018), *Essential Truths: The Bay Area in Color* (Pease Press, 2021), *Patrice Lumumba: An Anthology of Writers on Black Liberation* (Nomadic Press, 2021), and *the body has memories* (Nomadic Press, 2022). She writes about intergenerational healing by exploring what it means to heal from diasporic displacement as manifested in the body. Exploring themes of memory and loss, her work celebrates the ability of the physical and spiritual body to heal. Some of adrienne's favorite poets include Lucille Clifton, Patricia Smith, Nikki Giovanni and Tyehimba Jess. When she is not writing, adrienne is reading or watching documentaries. She also leads a healing writing circle for Black writers. More information about her work can be found at www.adriennedanyelle.com.

www.ingramcontent.com/pod-product-compliance
Lightning Source LLC
LaVergne TN
LVHW041510070426
835507LV00012B/1464